What PUPPIES Do Best

By Laura Numeroff  Illustrated by Lynn Munsinger

McGraw Hill Education

Puppies can wake you up in the morning,

try to climb onto your bed,

and give you a kiss.

Puppies can chase a ball,

learn how to sit,

and give you their paw.

Puppies can dig holes
in the yard,

track mud into the house,

and make a big mess.

Puppies can greet you
when you get home,

and roll over for a belly rub.

Puppies can go on walks,

make friends with other puppies,

and run alongside you!

Puppies can play tug-of-war,

take a bath,

and get you all wet.

Puppies can snuggle with you,

get cozy in their bed,

and give you a kiss good night!

But best of all . . .

puppies can give
you lots and lots
of love.

mhreadingwonders.com